WELCOME TO

UPLIFT

CHAPTER ONE

ANTON BROWN

Publisher

Welcome To Uplift

New York, NY 10001

Copyright © 2026 Anton Brown

ISBN (Paperback)

ISBN (Hardback)

ISBN (eBook)

This can be one of the longest dedications ever, because there's a countless number of individuals that deserve credit when it comes to who I am and what I stand for. The most high will always come first. I must give a special thank you to my cousin Denise Patrick Gant (Niece), who's more like an aunt and a sister. On Tuesday September 26, 2023 at 6:46 am she told me that I am the author of a motivational book and to make it happen immediately, she spoke those words into my life and told me it shall come to pass, she went on to say "I love you and when that book drop I'm going to be overjoyed". I want to say thank you to my cousin, I didn't see her vision then, but I see it now. If you all feel how I feel about this book, you can say thank you to her as well. I dedicate this book to you all, the people. Listening and seeing what we're all faced with encouraged me to be a voice that can spread to all at once, and this book gave me the opportunity to do that. Big thank you to my Mom and Dad for always persevering, my Grandmother(rip), Hama, and Hampa(rip) for always supporting me. Thank you to all my brothers, sisters, cousins, aunts, uncles, and to all that have supported me over the years; you know who you are.

A special shout out to my daughter, my son in law, and my son who inspires me everyday

Author's Note

I wrote this book with the intention of letting others know the words and feelings that came to me every day. I only shared this with my loved ones and people that I knew would be inspired by it or understand it. Some were combative of my thoughts or my studies, but to be honest, I was always aiming these words towards myself and what I needed in life at the time and now. I would study nightly and listen to messages daily while on my 9 to 5, and anything that stood out to me, I made sure to write it down, and some of these are my own creative thoughts that would just enter my mind at any given time. Every morning between 4 am and 6 am I would send these exact messages out through text. Prior to me beginning to send these messages out, I would just write them down and keep them to myself. Then I read this book by Ryan Leak titled Leveling Up, highly recommended. This book opened my eyes to sharing these thoughts and messages that I was only sharing with myself, with others, and that's how this all began. Once I saw the majority of my family and friends encouraged by my morning messages, I realized why not share these with the world. If you know me, then you know I love to encourage and uplift people; it provides me with self-gratification. I would hear certain messages and dissect them and put them into my own words.

It began to make sense to me, so I'm hoping by the end of this book, it will all make sense to you. Welcome to uplift!!!!

You're Rich And Wealthy

Every day

Of course, like many, most of us think of finances, the big house, the fanciest cars, high-priced jewelry, and the list goes on when we hear the words rich and wealthy. I can honestly say we're all rich and wealthy every day. To be rich in love, rich in forgiveness, rich in patience, rich in learning, rich in understanding, rich in your title such as a mother, a father, a daughter, a son, a sister, a brother, a cousin, a friend, an uncle, or an aunt, is one of the most amazing ways to be rich. That list can go on forever; you add some of your own ways to be rich, other than in finances.

To be wealthy in honesty, integrity, knowledge, fairness, camaraderie, perseverance, and uplift are just a few ways to be wealthy other than finances. What I'm basically saying is find ways to be rich and wealthy in areas that make you happy, as well as others. Doing this will bring about such a glow that others will probably think you're rich and wealthy just from your persona. I have always fought hard to be rich and wealthy in happiness and optimism. I'm not saying I have not ever been upset or mad, but as I stated, I have always fought hard for happiness and optimism, which can lead you to being rich and wealthy in peace, which is something else you should want to be rich and wealthy in. So always understand that being rich and wealthy don't always have to do with finances and the finer things, because to be honest, the finer things are inside of you.

Keep Being Strong

Keep Being Awesome

Keep Being Ferocious

Keep Going After All You

Want. Claim it Without Fear

Or Worry. Worry Is Faith

Turned Inside Out.

These words really mean a lot to me; I must tell myself and remind myself every day of these exact words. I would encourage you to do the same. Being strong all the time is not an easy task, but it's a mandatory task. To make it in this world, you must be strong; your strength will lead you right into awesomeness. Being awesome is something you will have to define for yourself.

I can say for me, though, that being awesome is guiding others in a beautiful direction. Helping others is something that I thrive on; it gives me a feeling of fulfillment. Now, when it comes to being ferocious, I don't mean this in a violent way, but I do mean it in an aggressive way. When you're going after your dreams, goals, and aspirations, you must go after them in a ferocious manner, attack, give it all you have, show that side of you that means business, losing isn't an option, and fear isn't an option. Fearing" means you have no faith. Hebrews chapter 11 verse 1 now faith is the substance of things hoped for, and the evidence of things not seen. I don't care what you're facing on this journey; don't ever face it with fear. If fear is something that keeps you bottled in, release it and know that you have everything it takes to make it.

Beautiful You Are

A lot of you might not believe this, but I have never, ever, one time in my life called anyone ugly, and that is a fact. You can't tell me that every individual walking on this earth isn't beautiful. Beauty comes in so many different forms. I've seen the most beautiful people on the outside, not so beautiful in their ways, attitude, and consideration.

When I look at people, I look at the all-around individual and not just the shell. I tend to use words such as they have such a beautiful personality, a beautiful heart, a beautiful work ethic, a beautiful concern for others, a beautiful approach, a beautiful way to redirect things, a beautiful way of learning, a beautiful way of listening, a beautiful way of loving, and that list goes on.

Beauty comes in so many different categories; it's almost to an infinite extent. I don't even like the word ugly, but if I had to use it, I would say the only thing that can make a person ugly is their attitude, and I would still find a way to call that person beautiful. Imagine looking at a 2-year-old baby painting and calling it ugly, that's that 2-year-olds creation, so how could we dare not find our creator's creation beautiful? Always remember how beautiful you are!!!!

People don't care how
much you know, until they know
how much you care...

It's so important to show individuals that you care. Caring can sometimes be just as valuable as love, because caring leads to love. There are so many people in the world who just gloat about how much they know or what they know, and that's fine and dandy, but it's so important to let people know you care. One way to let people know you care is by sharing what you know with them. When you share your knowledge and information with others, especially when it's beneficial, it allows others to know that you care in ways that are unexplainable. Giving knowledge and information is way more beneficial than giving presents or money.

Believe me, people know when you're looking out for them with care, the same way you know when people are looking out for you with care. When someone knows that you care, they will give you their all, and yes I know sometimes you can give your care to individuals and it's not as accepting as you may want it, but that's when you decipher who's worthy of your care and who's not, but to be honest, I always feel like everyone is worthy of my care, that's why I give it. Let's be transparent for a second. In 2013, I was robbed by someone very close to me, and of course, that wasn't the most exciting time of my life, but I can honestly say I still care about that person right now today, and they know it by my actions.

I say that, to say this, it allows others to care about how much you know by showing them how much you care.

Just Because They Don't Know What You Defeated, Don't Mean You Didn't Defeat It

There are always people looking from the outside who have no access to the inside. Sometimes it's good to keep your victories to yourself, it allows you to enjoy the fruits of it without anyone's opinion of how he or she did that, or sometimes they go as far as he or she didn't do that, there's no way, while the whole time you know what you overcame and how you overcame it. Overcoming things is always a form of defeating whatever it was that stood in your way.

When others haven't yet defeated their own shortcomings, they will tend to look at you as if there's no way you did. I have seen that happen plenty of times over my years. Always be proud of your defeats. The little ones can sometimes hold more weight than the big ones. You'll be surprised. Some people like to brag about their defeats. I've always respected humble people. Being humble just says so much about an individual; it speaks volumes about their character. I will always suggest being humble-

Passive by approach, restraint in your ways will always allow you to say, just because they don't know what I defeated, doesn't mean I didn't defeat it. Keep defeating all that's set-in front of you. If people knew my childhood and what I defeated, their eyes would get big, and their mouths would be wide open. We'll save that for another book, but I came out the victor. So always remember that you are the victor.

Be Patient With Your Process

This is very important. I learned this from a very prominent individual in the United States of America. He said don't rush your process and that's how this came to my mind. It stood out to me so vividly. I automatically thought be patient with your process and then I heard another prominent individual say exactly what I thought, "Be Patient With Your Process." When I heard him say this, I knew I was on to something and that I was thinking like the elites, because I consider these individuals' elites.

Vex King is someone who I would say is worthy of looking into. I would recommend checking out his work. He's a very encouraging and powerful individual. He's the one who stated don't rush your process and I had already thought to myself to be patient with your process, and then I listened to a T.D. Jake's message, and he stated, be patient with your process. I couldn't believe what I was hearing. I had already written this down prior to it; it kind of blew my mind, but I know that the mystery works in mysterious ways.

It's important to know that if you're not where you want to be, don't stress it or worry about it. It's your process, and it's going to work itself out. Put your work in and watch it work.

Reader's Thoughts

Silence Tomorrow

This is something that might not sound as uplifting, but believe me, it is. As human beings, we tend to worry about the future more than we do in the present time. I don't care what anyone says; the present time is the most important time you can have. The reason I say this is because the present develops the future, and it developed the past; don't let that go over your head. The present controls the narrative; that's why it's important to silence tomorrow.

Allow yourself to take care of what's important today, and tomorrow's importance will come. I won't ever say the future isn't important, because it is, but please understand that it's what you do today that matters the most. Perfect example, you have an assignment due tomorrow for work, school, etc. The reason you need to silence tomorrow is that the work must be done today. Knowing the present time is your time, perform at your best in every present time that you're granted.

I just want you to know that you're strong enough to mute everything other than your present time, and you can choose to mute your present time, but I can guarantee you it will lead you into a place where you're behind on everything you want. You're 100% built to accumulate all you want; I guarantee you that. The past can't do anything for you but teach you if you allow it to, and the future can't do anything for you if you don't take advantage of your presence in the present time. Go be Awesome by making tomorrow silent and taking advantage of your present time.

Reader's Thoughts

____

____

____

____

____

____

____

____

____

____

If You Don't Control
Your Own Time, Somebody
Else Will

It's one thing to be patient with your process, which we just spoke about on the previous page, but it's a whole other ball game to know the worth of your time. When you're using your time wisely, I would highly recommend being patient with your process. Now, when you're feeling like your time isn't yours, that's when it's time to take a step back to see what or who is getting more of your time than you. When you're focused on a goal, task, project, or anything of that nature, it's important to divide your time in a well-effective manner. Controlling your time is important because there's always something that someone else would either want or need you to do.

There's nothing wrong with helping others, as I stated earlier; that's one of my favorite things to do. You must realize that if the help you give to others is postponing your goals or dreams, it's time to measure what's more important. Now, in some cases, helping others may be worth putting off some things you have in store, but I can guarantee that that's not always the case. You must realize when others are controlling your time. Perfect example, I'm a morning person, and my mornings are very important to me. I get up around 4 a.m. I pray, I work out, and I read before giving my

8 hours to corporate America. I would notice just about every morning, I would have a family member or friend, mainly family members, *lol*, call me with the most obnoxious and unhappy conversations you would ever want to hear. It began to become depressing to me, to the point where I couldn't take it anymore. I had to realize I was allowing these people to control my time.

Before I knew it, it was 8 o'clock and time for me to go to work, and I hadn't got anything done, because I was giving my time to situations and circumstances that were not mine. After realizing that this was affecting my emotions. I had to politely ask people not to contact me in the morning, because that's a very special time for me and the things I would like to do. My advice to you is to pay close attention to when your time is being taken from you and how it's being taken from you, especially if you have dreams and aspirations. One last example, imagine if your favorite sports player or entertainer allowed his or her family or friends to interrupt their practice time, you would not have ever gotten to see their greatness and full potential. Go get what's yours by controlling your time.

Accept Uncertainty

It Shows Faith

By no means is this a religious book. I respect and understand that we all have our own beliefs; however, I do know that there are over 4,000 faith-based religions. I also know that faith is a belief system, so even atheists have faith. Uncertainty is something we all must encounter; no matter what our beliefs are, there is usually something that comes up in our lives that we're uncertain about. I can only share with you what works for me and pretty much assure you that it will work for you. I've seen it in action.

Accept the uncertainties, give your belief system that confidence that you know, however this works out, it's not going to keep you down or have a long-lasting effect on you and what you stand for, because I understand that all uncertainties don't always go our way. Accepting uncertainties allows your mind to slow down and your stress level to decrease.

It's basically telling the body it is what it is, and no matter what it is, we're going to be alright in the long run. That's faith unmeasured. If your uncertainties work out in your favor, you're a winner, and if they don't, knowing you're going to be alright in the long run still makes you a winner. Accept your uncertainties and keep pushing forward. You are the certainty!!

We Don't Surrender

We Don't Retreat

Every Man Must Search

His Own Soul...

To surrender means to retreat or to submit. I recommend you surrender and retreat when you search for your soul and you find it, when you're able to become the full you, erasing all the worldly things you've picked up along the way. Such as the habits, the ways, inaccurate thinking, and much more. Remember when you were born, you were born as pure as you can be. So, while on this journey, I will tell you not to surrender and not to retreat to any hardships, any obstacles, or any challenges. Continue to search for yourself, and when you find your pure self, I'm sure you will be very pleased.

Sometimes Getting
Better Hurts, Improvement
Is Healing

I'm pretty sure most of us, if not all, have been hurt before. Through experience, we can say that hurt is not a good feeling, because it's not. That moment you tell yourself, "You know what, I'm going to come out a better and stronger person after this," is the moment your healing will begin. Now most of us will pertain this to love or even injury, in which there's nothing wrong with that. We can admit when you're in love, and you get hurt; the healing process is, of course, an improvement to your mind, heart, and emotions. When you're injured, the physical therapy part is, of course, a healing process for improvement to the injured area or areas, but I tend to use this for another definition. When you're getting better as a person, it can sometimes hurt in many ways, such as having to give up habits that might put you through withdrawal, losing family members and friends because you don't do what they do anymore. Hearing people talk about you, saying you've changed or you're acting funny now that you're in the church or now that you don't smoke or drink any more, can sometimes hurt. The moral of the story is to allow yourself to get better, no matter how much it hurts, remember improvement is healing. So, continue to improve and get better.

Miracles Can Happen

Without Money

This is something that we would not ever be able to understand. That is why a lot of people think they need money to create miracles, but we all know miracles come from the supernatural and your faith, which once again is your belief system. I want to share a story with you all, allow me to be transparent, and please don't judge me (LoL). Ok, so I was locked up, yes, in jail in this small cell for 23 hours, I could only come out for one hour a day to shower and do whatever else it is I chose to do within the rules of the jail. While out for this one hour, I went to this book stand they had, and I found this book by Oral Roberts called the Miracle of Seed-Faith. Of course, I recommend you read it. I read this book in its entirety. While in my cell, I kept hearing another inmate scream out how cold he was and could he get an extra blanket, which of course they didn't give him. So, I'm lying on my bunk, and suddenly, the Correctional Officer comes through my loudspeaker and says Brown, "You're being released. Get all your stuff together. She popped my cell door and told me to follow her. I immediately stopped her and said ma'am can you please allow me to give the young man across from me my sweatshirt, I noticed he said he was cold in his cell. She said, "Are you sure, I said yes. She turned around, went behind her desk, and called his loudspeaker to ask if he was up, because it was close to midnight. He said, "Yes, why? What's going on"? She told him I'm going to open your door because somebody wants to give you something. She opened his door, and I approached him and said, "I would like to give you this. I noticed you telling the officers that you're cold at night". He was very accepting and appreciative of the shirt. Now, mind you, I was unable to get out of jail because I had absolutely no money at the time to bond out, but a bail bondsman who owned the company trusted me to pay him later, so he sent one of his bail bondsmen to get me. Once I was released into the bail bondsman's hands, I told him, "Look, man, I'm going to get you guys that $700 immediately". He looked at me and said, "Keep this between me and you, this one is on me, don't worry about that $700, just stay away from this place, man". I couldn't believe it; I didn't know this guy from nowhere. I didn't give that guy my sweatshirt to reap such a reward; I gave it to him out of generosity and from my heart. It was just amazing that that $20 sweatshirt paid for a $700 bail bondsmen bill, and so ironic that I had just read an Oral Roberts book about Sowing seeds. Miracles are everywhere, and that was a miracle to me; some might count it small, but I counted it big. I'd like to give a shout out to all the people who had bad doctor reports just to go back to the doctor and be told you're perfectly fine there's nothing wrong anymore (miracle), to the couples that was told they couldn't conceive but they did (miracle), to the people that were told they only had x amount of time to live and lived pass that (miracle), to the people that was told they would never see again, but they see now (miracle), and to everyone else that has experienced a miracle. Go get your miracle, make that belief system so strong that it's undeniable.

Reader's Thoughts

———————————————————————————

———————————————————————————

———————————————————————————

———————————————————————————

———————————————————————————

———————————————————————————

———————————————————————————

———————————————————————————

———————————————————————————

———————————————————————————

You're Not Ever Improved,
Even When You've Improved
#WEALWAYSGETTINGBETTER!

Some people tend to reach a level of improvement and consider that their maximum capacity. Well, I'm here to tell you otherwise. There's no level of improvement that can be too high; improvement is measured on an infinity scale. I'm a firm believer that improvement can't be measured as long as you want to keep improving. Now, if you don't want to keep improving, yeah, you can stay stagnant, but who would want to do that besides a complacent person? I have nothing against complacent people, because some people are satisfied with where they are. I just want to let you know that if you're not satisfied, don't ever allow yourself to be stuck. Being complacent and being stagnant are forms of being stuck, and this can sometimes come from lack of motivation or lack of enthusiasm; in which, I've been down those roads, but I put my boxing gloves on and fought that. So, if you feel like you can improve more, which I know you can. Put your boxing gloves on and knock complacency and stagnancy out of the box.

#STAYINMOTIONWEALWAYSGETTINGBETTER

Live Like Nobody Else
So You Can Live Like
Nobody Else

This can be tricky, but it's not tricky. If you really look at the world, and I mean really look at the world. This world is a simultaneous world; everyone's doing the same thing, like seriously, everyone is really doing the same thing. Now, there are a few people who step outside that box, and that's who I'm talking about, but I want the people who know they are doing the same thing to pay attention to this as well. Everyone's smoking weed, everyone's drinking until they can't drink anymore, everyone's getting girls, getting guys, everyone's gossiping, everyone's on social media, and I can keep going if you want me to. If you can recall, and some of you might not be able to, but in the 80's when crack cocaine hit, everyone was doing crack. It's sad how we follow the world and end up living like the world. What I'm saying to you is build your path differently, because if you pay attention to the patterns that everyone else is following, they all are getting the same results, and I was once on that ship; nevertheless, getting the same results. Money is low, living check to check, don't own a home, building bad habits in my children through my actions without even knowing that's what I was doing, priorities upside down, now this one wasn't an issue for me, but it is for a lot of people waiting for tax time to come just to have something. This list can be very long. So really comprehend what this passage says and live like nobody else, so you can live like nobody else. You're worthy of owning a home, you're worthy of going on a family vacation whenever you want, you're worthy of having big savings, to be honest, you're worthy of it all, so do what the passage says, and it will serve you well. It took me a long time to understand this.

If Somebody Has To

Lose, It's Not Gonna

Be Me

This is the approach we must take in everyday life, like for real. If you look back over the time you have spent on this earth, I'm sure you can look and see that you have taken more than enough losses. Well, at least I can look back over my time here and say enough is enough; I've taken one too many losses. That's what triggered this quote in my head: the losses I've taken, and there's nothing wrong with taking losses; it's life lessons, but we don't want to keep on losing. I'm sorry, but I don't want you to keep on losing. So, carry this with you and say it to yourself often. Begin to strategically plan things out that you know are going to work in your favor. That's what I began to do, and it's been working for me. I can honestly say I haven't taken a loss in a while once I set my mind on this. You're a winner, and the reason I know that is because you were built to win.

It's Time To Do
Some Stuff That You Don't
Feel Like Doing

This can go hand in hand with live like nobody else, so you can live like nobody else if you really think about it, because to do that, you have to do some things that you might not feel like doing. Perfect example, remember having homework to do and some of you may still have homework to do, but remember not wanting to do it, although it was going to benefit you in the long run, remember not wanting to go to work and some of you probably still don't feel like going to work, but we know that's what pays our bills. I'm just saying, really weigh out what it is you know you can do or things you should be doing that's going to help you, help your family, etc. Go do it, the world is in your hands. Stop putting it off. I didn't feel like writing this book, but guess what, I did it. I have a grandson now; I must do a lot of things that I may not feel like doing for the sake of him and me (of course, the rest of my family too). I'm sure you all have special people in your lives that's worth doing some things that may be challenging or may be a headache, but for their sake, go get it done. I believe in you.

Everything You Do Has A Value To It

First off, we must know the definition of value and the importance of that word. To value something is to hold something at a high standard; it shows that you're worthy, that you're beneficial. Everything we do has an impact. Not only are you valuable, but your actions are just as valuable as you. Good deeds don't ever go unnoticed; they add to your value. That's something I've always instilled in my children as they grew up. It never hurts to do good by people, even if they don't do good by you; it shows great morals and values. I can honestly say that I didn't always live by this. Perfect example being a young man hanging out on the corner smoking and drinking, and this is not me judging anyone, it's me judging me, but that did nothing for my value, it decreased my value if you let me tell it. I had to buckle down and tell myself you're too valuable for that. It was one incident that happened that made me look in the mirror and know that everything I do has value to it. I came home one day, and my grandmother (Alberta Brown) called me into the kitchen. She stated that one of her friends saw me on the corner drinking. I didn't feel bad about it, but I can tell my grandmother did. She was disappointed, she said, "Now come on, Brown, you're better than that baby, you're an honor roll student in college getting your degree, that takes away from who you really are." Now, my grandmother wasn't saying that I was better than anybody else; she was just letting me know my worth. From that day, I vowed never to be on the corner drinking. She went on to say there's nothing wrong with you having a drink, because it isn't what you do, it's how you do it, and being on that corner is not it. Coming from me, Anton Brown, I want you to know that you were made wonderfully special and that your value is out of this world.

Rest And Wait For The Mystery To Reveal The Next Step, To Provide The Next Weapon And The Next Strategy

Although I'm a believer, I'm always cautious of others' beliefs, so instead of using God, I tend to use the mystery a lot, just out of respect for non-believers. This quote can be a hard one, but if you know that there's a strength out there greater than yours than this is for you. We all sometimes run into situations that are out of our control, but we still try to control them. When we sit back and relax our minds in times of chaos, this is exactly what we should be resting our minds on, allowing that higher power to work it out, trusting and knowing that it's going to all fall right in place. Now the word weapon is not defined as a gun, knife, or anything of that nature in this passage, but instead it's relating to the resources that will be provided to you to approach the strategy and take the next steps you need to get to where you're going, noticed I said where you're going and not where you're trying to go. I'm telling y'all this really works. Back in 2014, I couldn't get a job for nothing, no matter what I did, they were just refusing me left and right. I knew I had a record, so of course that didn't help. I'm just realizing today that this entered my life way back then. I had to sit down, I had to rest, and I had to wait. This is a true story. I was brushing my teeth one Sunday before church, and this voice kept talking to me, telling me to put x amount of dollars in church that day, remember I'm unemployed. I'm going to be honest, I fought with that voice and said there's no way I'm putting that much money in nobody's church, and we went back and forth, back and forth. To the point, I said no. I got in the car to leave, and it got louder to the point that I couldn't resist it, and we were already backing out of the driveway. I had to stop the car and go back inside and get that money. Mind you, I didn't know this was the next step that was going to give me my weapons and reveal to me the strategy. Honest Truth, I put that money in the offering plate that Sunday, and on that Monday, I got two job offers. Both jobs told me that I can't work two jobs because their schedules are always different. Long story short, I worked both, the mystery made that happen, I worked from 7a.m. to 3:30p.m. on one and 4p.m. to 10p.m. on the other. I learned that day that you must rest and wait for the mystery to reveal itself. I'm telling you don't ever let your mind trick you to believing it's over or it can't be done, because how you're designed is like no other, you're designed for greatness.

Making A Decision Is Always Better Than Not Making A Decision. At least If You Make The Wrong Decision, It Carries Grace And A Lesson

I'm not perfect, and I'm sure none of you are either. Deciding can sometimes be hard, and we don't always make the right decisions, but it's ok, at least a decision was made, that's how I feel. People tend to beat themselves up when they make the wrong decision. I would recommend you not, because we're all out here learning. Every wrong decision I've made, I made sure to remember it, not do it again, and share it with the people I love, so if they're ever faced with it, they can make the right decision, that's grace alone right there; that's divine assistance at its best, helping others to not make the same mistakes you did. Learning lessons is one of the most awesome things you can do, yea I know nobody likes to learn a lesson, but boy, if it doesn't teach you. I'm thankful for every lesson I had to learn and thankful for the grace that followed behind it. I just want you to know that you're so covered you can afford to make a mistake occasionally, make the wrong decision once in a while, none of us are perfect, but we're all worth it.

You're Gonna
Get There And When
You Do, You Will Be
Presented Faultless

We work so hard every day as citizens of this country; some of us work towards something, some of us just work to work. Well, I'm here to tell you if you're working towards something, you will get there and if you're working to work, we'll see you at retirement. We all know there's nothing picture perfect on this journey we're all on. There will be some things that will work hard to discourage you and encourage you to quit, slam the gavel, say it's over, and I'm done. That attitude will either have you behind or at a standstill. No matter what you do, if you're doing it from your heart with pure intentions, you will be presented faultless, and your reward will not be presented lightly; it will be presented as if you're walking the red carpet. That's what gets us there, working for and from our hearts and not just for the rewards. When we work from our hearts it's a certain protection that's placed over us and our work to the point that people can say no to your work every day, all day, but in due time, they'll see that their no should've been a yes. When that happens, that's your evidence that you have been presented faultless.

Whatever It Is, Don't Give In.

Fight it, Resist It, War Against It,

Eventually you're going to get The

Victory

This is the art of war, the art of war at its best. This is what you must prepare for over the years you may have wasted or the years that you weren't as successful or active as you may have wanted to be. I'm telling you, I'm not sure how many of you have ever been in a physical fight, this is it right here. This fight is way worse than a physical fight. I've been in many, and this mental fight is way more challenging than a physical fight, I'll take a physical fight any day, I'm telling y'all know stories. I would physically fight for my wisdom every single day if that's what I had to do to retain it. And I'm whipping tale for that (4real). When you can fight it, war against it, and resist it, that's when you know your wisdom is being uprooted.

As Long As You're

Seeking You're

Never Lost

To seek is to find, especially when you have a strong belief system. There's no getting lost when you're seeking. It's the people who stop seeking that tend to find themselves lost or confused. I would encourage every individual to continue to look for what you want, continue to look for a way out. Even if you don't know what you want or even if you don't see a way out, continue to seek, because that's the only way that you're going to find what you want or find that way out. If you're not seeking, then you're allowing yourself to be lost. So many people sit back and throw a pity party and wonder why they're lost or confused, well I can tell you it's because they gave up on seeking. Don't ever give up on seeking; it's going to get you right where you need to be.

Mercy Is So Great

That It'll Often Give You

What You Didn't Deserve

As we all know, mercy is a form of forgiveness, and it's not just any form of forgiveness. It's a form of forgiveness that spares an individual. Most of the time, mercy is used when someone has done something wrong that's deserving of punishment. Mercy is sparing one from punishment. The reason I love this saying is that it's true. I want you all to think back to a time when you knew you did something wrong, but instead of you being punished for it, it turned into a blessing or a life learning experience that wasn't punishing. I can date back to a time when my brothers and I, and when I say my brothers, I mean my true brothers that I'm still together with today, me personally, I don't have any friends. We weren't even 20 years old yet, and we would get drunk, high and go into adult clubs that we weren't even supposed to be in, but we had fake identification cards. So, one night we were all out partying and we had a run in with a group of individuals that was all 28 and older. One of them knew that one of my brothers was having an affair with his wife, so immediately he swung at my brother. Of course, we got into a big brawl in this club, and before I knew it, the whole club was empty, and it was just me, my best brother, and the guy who threw the first punch at my other brother. He brandished a gun, and he just stood there pointing it at us.

Mind you, this had nothing to do with us; we weren't the ones having an affair with his wife. Our brother was, although we're going to fight for each other no matter what. My best brother was in a state of shock; he was bleeding out of his mouth at an alarming rate. As I tapped him on his leg and whispered under my breath to him, "On the count of three were going to run," he heard nothing. I got to three and he walked off while I ran. The gunman ran after me. I kept running, but I'll not ever in my life forget the fire coming out of that gun as he shot at me and the look of evil all over his face. I just looked back, not understanding how I wasn't shot yet. He aimed every shot right at me. I know I have stated numerous times that this isn't a religious book; in which, it's not, but I'll be the first to tell y'all it was God that saved us that night. He had his mercy all over us. Think about it, we're out drinking, doing all types of adult things that we didn't have any business doing, and then we end up with a gun in our face, and I end up being shot at. For all the wrong things we had done that night, mercy was still showered upon us. I can't say we didn't deserve to walk away from that alive, but I can say that we were playing on the devils' playground, and it could have cost us. That's why I say mercy is so great that it'll often give you what you didn't deserve, just pay attention and know how and when to count your blessings.

The Ability To

Do The Opposite

Of Those Against You

Provides Elevation

This is a funny one, yet a good one. We want to all think there's no one against us or not for us, well, I don't think I'm being the bearer of bad news, but believe me, there's always someone lurking in the cut not agreeing with you and what you bring forth. Now there are some people who truly believe everyone loves them and is all for them (I tend to be one of those people smh), I give my props to them and hope it works out, good luck!! You know how I survived this and still survive it; I'm giving away something that I'm not perfect at, but it has gotten me further than it didn't. I have always approached every situation, no matter how bad, with the most positive attitude and approach possible, now when I was younger, I didn't do this. I got to be honest, but try it, please, just approach every situation with the most positive approach you can give. Nothing negative and when I say nothing negative, nothing negative at all. To be able to forgive someone at a higher level, to be able to do no harm to someone that may want to do harm to you, to have the ability to not say one malice word against anyone that has a malice word against you, the ability to uplift them in any way you can find possible is a perfect way to accept your elevation.

Just Because They
Look At You As The Least
Doesn't Mean You're The
Less

To be less means to be low in quantity, that alone should let you know that you're not the least and you're sure enough not less. Quantity couldn't dare walk in quality shoes, and your quality. I have a friend who's blind (she has passed on since I wrote this book, I miss you, Shelly~) and she shared with me some of the most awful things that she has experienced coming from other human beings as a blind woman. Some of the things others have said to her, I just couldn't believe. They look at her as the least because she's blind. Some may feel as if her presence isn't quality enough for them, because she may be limited in some areas, well I'm here to be the first one to tell you, this young lady would light up a room and bring so much fun and laughter to the table. To be honest, there aren't many people I know that can work a room with such charisma, with such a positive attitude and outlook on everything. I can honestly say she's the true definition of this, because although they may look at her as the least, she sure enough is not less. Make sure you know every day that least and less is nowhere near equivalent to you and that what you carry is more than enough.

We Really Don't Know Anything Until We Realize We Don't Know Anything

To know everything would be awesome, or would it? We all go through this system of education; in which it symbolizes a form of preparation. We conquer this system just to graduate, walk into the real world, and realize that we don't know anything, of course I'm not speaking to the know it all's right now. This is where the real preparation comes in at. I must be honest, that's when I realized I didn't know anything. I graduated college on the dean's list Grade point average looking great, just to find out that I have a whole lot of learning to do. I knew nothing and I'm so thankful that, I knew I knew nothing. One thing to always remember is that your cup is never full. One thing I remember telling my son during his first week of college was "Son, you're not here to know, you're here to learn". When this topic came to my mind of course I wrote it down and sent it out in one of my morning texts. I got a response back from a friend and it was a Socrates quote that I had not ever seen before the quote said, "The only thing I know, is that I know nothing". Of course, my mind was blown, because who am I to think like Socrates, one of the greatest philosophers to walk the planet? I'm not going to discount myself too much, but it was a

WOW!! Moment. When things like that happen to me, I pay close attention, it tends to be a whisper from the universe if you let me tell it. When you realize that you don't know anything, learning will become a hobby. Always remember you don't know anything, until you realize you don't know anything.

It's Less Of What

You Did And

More Of What You

Don't Do

Some people get so caught up in all the negative things they have done that they tend to forget there are still more positive things that can be done. As we get older on this earth, I feel it's important to pay attention to what it is that you're not doing to get yourself in a position to form the victory stance. What you did holds no weight anymore and if there are people holding on to that, leave them that bag; you keep it pushing. What you don't do leaves the door open for people to dwell on what you did do; it even leaves the door open for you to dwell on it. We've all done things that we're not proud of but just remember what you don't do will have a stronger effect on your future than what you did do. This is solely for people who beat themselves up for what they did. Leave what you did alone and go get yours. It's waiting for you. Like Nike Just do it!!!

You Have Done More

With A Little Than People Have

Done With A Lot

I love this, the reason being is because I have literally seen this with my own eyes my whole life. Coming from where I come from, it's hard, it's tough, and there are so many other individuals that come from the same background. I have watched drug dealers pull out big wads of money, just to find out they don't take care of their children. I have been connected to some very rich people over my days, just to watch them not want to give. I have seen people with the most do the least, and people with the least do the most. I love it because it tells you a lot about a person. I have brothers who coach Pop Warner football in high-poverty areas, and when I tell you my brothers do so much for these children, it's amazing and they do it with little or nothing, but the children don't know that, and my brothers don't ever complain or show them that. I've seen them give their last to the organization, I've seen them in the streets asking for donations, I've seen them feeding these children before they feed themselves, and this list can go on. Now this is a perfect example of this topic. I had an uncle, an awesome guy pastor, a leader, very wealthy, but you would have had to pay him to get a dollar from him. He had maids, butlers, drivers, the whole nine yards. I can't say my uncle didn't do good deeds for others, but I can assure you there was a lot more he could've done. Not putting him down, because that was my man, sometimes you just look, observe, and learn the ways of others(I must say he did what the most high put him here to do, who am I to say what he was supposed to do). I have a very rich friend who, on thanksgiving was only feeding his immediate family, and when I say immediate, I mean immediate. No cousins, no aunts, no uncles, maybe one brother, but the other siblings could kick rocks. I was lucky to be the only friend one thanksgiving. And then I look at my grandmother, and I don't know how she did it. We would have the biggest thanksgiving's ever off a security guard's salary with no food stamps. When I say my grandmother fed every family member, every friend of every family member, their friends, girlfriends, she basically fed the entire Newburgh, NY, no stories. When I look back as an adult, I always question how she did so much with so little and we all even used to have leftovers to take home for real, y'all. Not only did we have leftovers, but we would also eat at her house for the entire week after our leftovers were gone, it was insane. Please, and I'm begging, please don't ever look at your situation as if you're not capable, when you don't have, be sure to do more. I don't care how much you have or don't have; just know you can do it.

You Don't Need
The Past, To Feel
Good About The
Future

I'm going to put it like this, what's done is done, and what's not done has got to get done. One thing we can say is that our future is not ever done, we live for the future, not the past. If you have not yet organized your life, guess what? If you're reading this book, you still have time to organize it. That's what I mean by we don't need the past to feel good about the future. I guarantee you, as soon as you begin to line things up for your future, it's going to feel so good, once again we don't need our past to feel good about our future. I know someone that went to college straight out of high school, but it didn't work for them. They ended up dropping out. That same person is 41 years old and about to graduate from school this year to become a psychologist now tell me if that's not the definition of you don't need the past to feel good about the future. I know someone else who didn't know what they wanted to do with their life, was out doing about every drug you can think of. At the age of 28 this person decided to enlist in the Army. Did a few years in the Army, they came home and decided they wanted to get a bachelor's degree and went on after that bachelor's degree to get a master's degree. Right now, as I type, that person is working for the Government. Another perfect example is that you don't need your past to feel good about your future. I don't care what you have done in the past, don't let it affect your future.

Reader's Thoughts

You Have The

Strength For

Any Struggle

Do this for me. Look back at your past struggles and then look at yourself in the mirror for a good 30 seconds. Now you tell me if you don't see strength, and the reason you should see strength is that those past struggles didn't wipe you out, even if some of them may have seemed victorious they weren't, because you're still out here stepping. The first thing is knowing and believing that you have the strength for any struggle. You may be going through a struggle right now, which means now is the time to talk to your strength. We were placed on this earth to face challenges and accept challenges. I don't think there's anyone that is on this earth or passed through this earth that wasn't faced with struggles. We all know you can have all the money in the world, but there is still something you will struggle with. Rest in peace, Richard Pryor, some of you may know him, and some of you may not. One thing I can say is that man made a lot of money over his career, but he struggled with drug addiction. It almost killed him numerous of times but see that's the perfect example right there that you have the strength for any struggle that man overcame every time because of his strength. I'm so thankful that man lived to get on stage and tell us his story. Not only did he tell us his story, he made it funny. So always keep it in your back pocket that you have the strength for any struggle.

Reader's Thoughts

____

____

____

____

____

____

____

____

____

____

There's Sometimes

Pain In The Words

I've Learned

Yes, this is an uplifting book, but we must remember when we're dealing with uplift, there's usually a pain, or a cause, or a problem that we're being uplifted for or from. I can recall many times I was down and out, and I would always say, "I need some uplift right now". We have all learned something and we know that learning isn't always fun. Some people have had to go to prison to use the words I've learned, some people have had to lose close loved ones or friends to use the words I've learned, and some people have had to go to rehab to use the words I've learned. These are all painful events and situations, but sometimes it takes that for us as people to understand and say I've learned. My closest brother, yeah, the one who was held at gunpoint with me, had to endure some pain to use the words I've learned. If anyone knows him, they will tell you he's one of the quietest, humblest, and most respectful young men you could ever meet. During some hard times in his life, he decided to try the drug game. It was a shock to everybody, believe me, but this decision landed him in prison for six years, which broke my heart. I could honestly say when my brother came home from that six-year sentence, he used the words I've learned and has not ever put himself in a situation like that again. So don't be afraid to use your pain to exemplify that you've learned.

Reader's Thoughts

You Have More
Power Than You've
Been Using

Power is a strong word, but what's so funny is that we all possess it. Some may sometimes feel like they're powerless, well I'm here to tell you that you're not ever powerless. It's a word that has been abused so much through action, that people don't even want power anymore. Well, I'm speaking on a power that is undeniable and has been granted to you since birth. I want you to know that you can speak power over yourself, you can speak power into your situations, you can speak power over your children, as well as other's situations. This goes back to your belief system. When you wake up in the morning you should know you have the power to face another day, the power to increase who you are and what you stand for. You know when I recognized that I had more power than I had been using; it was when I saw students disrespecting their parents and respecting me and then respecting me enough to begin to respect their parents. It was amazing having moms and dads come to me, like Mr. Brown I don't know what you said to my child but thank you. I haven't ever seen this behavior from my child before. Power is something we should all take seriously and use for the good of ourselves and others; it's a source that you were blessed with from day one. Use it!!!!!

There's No Greater
Me Than Me. I'm The
Best Me There Will Ever
Be

I'm about to sound confused, but y'all will get it. You might have to read it a couple times. There's a me and there's you. There's you and there's a me. When you look at you, you see a me and when I look at me, I see a me. I just want everyone to know that there's no greater you than you, and that you're the best you there will ever be. You were made unique and special in your own way. How could there ever be a greater you than you, it's impossible. So, it's extremely important every day to reach for the greatest you, because only you can do that. Reach for the best you, because you have the power to do that. I don't care how much people attempt to mimic others, remake songs, etc. now the remake of a song may sometimes sound better than the original but guess what the person who remade it could not ever be as good as the creator the originator and that's how there could be no greater them than them and there the best them that there will ever be, just because they were the originator, they came up with it, the person that remade it can't say they created it. So always know when you look in that mirror tell yourself there's no greater me than me and I'm the best me there will ever be.

Simplify Your

Pursuits

We all should have pursuits, something that we're pursuing, and if you don't, it's fine, just promise me you'll find something positive to pursue after reading this book. Right now, as I type, I'm pursuing becoming a best-selling author. To simplify simply means making something easier to make something understandable the best way possible. I'm going to use me as an example. I just shared with you all that I'm pursuing becoming a best-selling author. Now to simplify this pursuit, I had to turn my phone off, I had to become disciplined enough to come home after my 9 to 5 and write, I had to study every day, and on most days, I had to disconnect myself from the world. That was me simplifying my pursuit. It was easier for me to get things done this way, and that's all I'm saying, make things as easy as you can when you're pursuing what you're pursuing. It's only right, you owe that to yourself, to make things as easy as you can. Now I'm not saying the pursuit won't still be challenging, but at least you've done some things to make it a little easier on yourself. Some people may get upset with you that you don't have the time they feel they deserve, but that's when you must remember and remind yourself that this is about you and your pursuit. So, from here on out always remember to simplify your pursuits.

Hurt Could Equal

Correction

We have all been corrected a time or two or three, for that matter, but not everybody has allowed hurt to correct them. Some people may ask how you could put the two together. Well, here I am to explain my version. As we touched on earlier no one wants to be hurt that's no fun, but when you use hurt to correct something, it makes it all so better. I was in the streets for a long time, and boy, did that hurt my grandmothers, they basically lived on their knees due to my actions, so thankful for their prayers. I knew I was hurting my grandmothers, and that's what led to corrections. Sometimes we must look at the effects of the hurt and be mindful enough to allow it to equal correction. Their worry alone caused me to correct a lot of things; it wasn't my hurt, it was their hurt that equaled the correction. When I got out of the streets and saw the pride my grandmothers still had in me, that was one of the most beautiful lest corrections I could have ever made, and it all stemmed from their hurt. I'm excited to hear or read your version on how hurt equal correction.

People With The
Most Problems Are The
Answer

This is a very true statement. We all have problems, and most of the time we're looking around for the answer to our problems, not realizing we're the answer. If you look back at some of the problems you have faced, I bet 9 times out of 10 you came up with the solution, even if it was you reaching out to someone to help you with that problem; you still created a solution that was the answer to the problem. I have a cousin that I am very close to. For many years she had an addiction to crack cocaine. I can honestly say my cousin probably went to rehab 7 times, if not more. When I say my cousin had problems, she had problems. It was that last time she went to rehab, she came home and vowed to not ever go back to that drug. The whole time she was the answer, why do I say this, because why didn't it work the other 6 times she went. You want to know why; she didn't want it to work. It was when she decided it was over, it was over. That's how it goes with all of us, because to be honest most problems go in circles. People see themselves facing the same problems every month. When you realize the answer is in you, that's when those problems will be fixed in totality. Theres no one who can face your problems like you and answer every question that needs to be addressed. That's all it is with problems. It is asking yourself some questions and answering them honestly and truthfully, that's how you are the answer to your problems. So, the next time you have a problem or problems, just know that you are the answer.

Reader's Thoughts

____

____

____

____

____

____

____

____

____

____

Something Is Being
Worked Out That You
Don't Even Know About

As human beings, we tend to worry a lot; that's just the nature of a human. We would love for everything to be just right, but that's not always the case. I have to be honest, when I was young, I used to worry like crazy, no one knew this, but I did. I mainly worried about my mother. As I do a playback of my youth, things always seemed to work out. Getting older really shaped me into a non-worrying person; now I help and encourage people not to worry. I have had so many incidents that I've seen work out over the years, that I have really trained myself not to worry about anything. Rest assured as you read this something is being worked out that you don't even know about. I remember before I got my instructor position at an alternative school, I was so worried about my past being brought up and me not landing the position. Back then, I didn't know what I know now. So of course, I'm praying, telling the Great I Am that I won't sell another drug if I land this job. Long story short, I got the job and kept my word. I didn't even realize that something was being worked out that I didn't even know about. There's more to this story, but I'll save that for another time. Just always remember you have a power that is constantly working things out, no matter how bad it may look. Also remember not knowing about it being worked out is the fun part, because when it presents itself, it feels so good.

Reader's Thoughts

Sometimes The

Answer

Is In The Absence

When something is missing out of our lives, we sometimes look at it as if it doesn't matter, sometimes we think it's a bad thing, sometimes we think it's a good thing, and sometimes we want what's absent back. I'm here to tell you that sometimes the answer lies within whatever it is that's missing. People don't like to admit some things, but I'm going to admit this. I'm an alcoholic, I don't drink like I used to at this time, but I know that gene lies dormant inside of me. All the years I drank I hurt so many people, not to mention myself. Only if I knew the answer was in the absence. Once I stopped drinking so many things began to come together for me, so many good things. If I had known the answer was in the absence I would have stopped drinking a long time ago, but this goes back to some things are being worked out that you don't even know about. My cousin that I spoke about earlier in the book didn't know the answer was in the absence, she got off crack cocaine and is now a Certified Nurse's Aide, doing excellent for herself. It takes time, but eventually we end up finding out that sometimes the answer is in the absence. I don't speak much about my mother's issues because it's a very sensitive and touchy subject, but when my mother left her first husband, things just started coming together for her, and when she left her second one too. Oops!!! Sorry, ma, the answer was in the absence. You can associate this with so many different topics, that once again I'm excited to hear about or read what answer lies in the absence for you.

YOU OWE IT TO

YOURSELF

I touched on this topic a little bit when I spoke at my grandmother's funeral. We as individuals tend to not give ourselves enough props and props is what you're deserving of when you do good deeds, if you may not know what props is. We give everybody else their props, but forget about ourselves, I know I'm guilty of it. The reason I spoke about this at her funeral is because my grandmother did so much for the family and so much for others, but one thing I did not ever see or hear my grandmother do is give herself props, until her last year on this earth. For those of you that were at her funeral you heard this story, but for those of you that weren't this is how it went. Me and my grandmother were in her living room chopping it up like we do, for those of you that don't know what chopping it up means it just means talking. This was probably 5 weeks before her expiration. So, we were sitting around talking about education and my grandmother looked at me and said "Brown the only time I got to go to school is when it rained" I must be honest, that went over my head. I had to go home to think about it and call her and ask her what she meant by that. She told me that when it rained, she didn't have to be in the field; she said she used to have to watch all the children go to school every day unless it rained. That really sat on my heart how blessed we all are to be able to get our education and not be held back from getting our education. She went on to say, "Brown, I'm so proud of me, I did it on an eighth-grade education, I got me a state job, I retired, and I took care of all of y'all". My grandmother was talking about herself, I didn't ever hear my grandmother give herself props. It was so cool to hear the woman who raised me give herself props; she was deserving and worthy of that, she owed it to herself. After that day I told myself, I'm going to start acknowledging me more and I encourage you all to start acknowledging yourselves more. You're worthy of the acknowledgment. YOU OWE IT TO YOURSELF!!!!

Patience Can Calm

Down

A Lot Of Things

One of people's favorite sayings is "I'm running out of Patience". Don't run out of patience, run to more patience. Patience is a weapon, patience is a tool, patience is rest, patience is a powerful resource, that many of us don't use. Patience has saved so many situations and controlled so many outcomes. There's a lot of people still making it today because of their patience. It's a known fact that patience helps to decrease anxiety levels, and impatience helps to increase anxiety levels. One thing we should all want is a calm life, a calm expiring experience, calm friends with calm spirits. It plays such a major role in your everyday being. The fact that you have the ability to roam this earth composed, peaceful, without anger, worry, or excitement shows heavily that one knows how to control their thoughts and emotions. We all have this ability; the question is, do you have enough strength to use it? Of course, I would say you do, because I know you do. So now we have to answer another question, do you want to use your strength to exercise this ability? I think it's important to wake up every day and tell yourself, "I'm going to have patience with this day, no matter what attempts to interrupt my patience, I will not let it". Now I'm not saying don't get excited over things, because it's fun to get excited. I'm just saying don't allow your anxiety to get excited, don't allow your fear and worry to get excited. Control that with the strength you were born with. You got this, because believe me, it's a true fact that patience can calm down a lot of things, allow it to calm you.

Whatever Is Necessary

Is Possible

There are many things on this earth and in this universe that are necessary, and of all the things that are necessary we can't say we know how they all were created. That shows us right there that whatever is necessary is possible. A necessity is a requirement; when you're required to do something, you're always giving possibilities. You're required to graduate high school, you're giving possibilities to do so, you're required to make a living for yourself, you're giving possibilities to do so. When I see people panhandling in the streets, I always think of this because it's a necessity for them to get what they need whatever that may be and they make it possible by any means necessary. People always say "if you want to start a business find something that is necessary" basically find something that's needed, the reason they say this is because they know it's a strong possibility that you may become successful off the need of others. If you begin to dig deep and put some necessities on you, I guarantee you, you'll start seeing possibilities for those necessities begin to come out of nowhere. Yes, I like to give examples. I know someone that was living off somebody, I can't stand to say it, but they were leaching off someone. That person got kicked out of the home they were staying at. So, guess what, when that person got kicked out, it became a necessity for them to make a living for themselves. Right now, today that person has a nice place to stay, well-paying job, and beautiful children they're raising. I must say, without that necessity being put on them, there would not have ever been a possibility to acquire all that they have acquired since being asked to leave. Sometimes it takes you to put the necessities on you, and sometimes it takes others putting the necessities on you. Just know that whatever is necessary is possible. Go find a necessity and make it possible. There are other people that can be rewarded by you, making your necessity possible. That job you attend every day or went to every day was or is a necessity and you got rewarded by someone else, making it possible.

Protect What You've

Been Made A Steward Over

We have all been giving something that we're a Steward over, even if it's only your own life, you're in charge. Being a steward is receiving high responsibility, being of a high authority when it comes to household and family possessions, and sometimes it can be other people's possessions. When someone makes you a steward over something, they trust you, they know you can protect. To know that you have been made a steward is a beautiful thing. Before you even took your first steps as a child, you were already made a steward. I look at my grandson, and I see a steward all day; right now, he's being a steward over his pacifier. That boy protects that pacifier with all he has got, and please don't attempt to take it, because you're going to have a fight on your hands, I can tell you that (no more pacifier, he's 3 years old now and potty trained). It's amazing just knowing we're trusted with such a high-quality position. The next time you're not feeling in charge, remind yourself of what you're a steward over, like I said earlier even if it's just you, that's so important within itself. I know a homeless guy who wants to be homeless; he doesn't care to live under anyone's roof, but I guarantee you that everything he's been made a steward over is protected. His cleanliness is out of this world, hand washes his belongings every day, and he takes great care of his tent and toiletries that he has. He just shows his stewardship and gratefulness for what it is he's in charge of. It amazes me, and it keeps me in perspective, little do you know. Seeing him so actively taking care of what he's in charge of encourages me more than you guys would think. Let me tell you what's even crazier about this homeless man situation, he has made someone who attempted to give him a place to stay the steward over all his income, and she's not even related to him. Another thing that I love is that he's black and she's white, I love that. Yes, some homeless people collect income too. This lady does so right for him, and all he receives. Just imagine a homeless person making you the steward over all they collect. I just want you to always remember you were made worthy of stewardship before you were handpicked to be here. Trust yourself, because I know someone who trusts you.

What You Have

Built

Is Not Ordinary

If you can remember, at the beginning of this book, I stated that I would write these down and that I was aiming them at myself, until it came over me, to why not share this with the world. Well, this is one that I wrote down and knew people needed to know this; they need to hear and read this. I mean, I'm speaking of everyday normal living people like me that might not have a big house, fancy cars, etc., no knock on them, I'm happy for them. I'm sure they look around and know what they have built is not ordinary, but all of us need to understand that what we have built is not ordinary, because a lot of us have survived some things that others haven't, and we're still building. That's the part right there, still building. It doesn't matter if you're sleeping on your friend's couch, in your parents' place right now, a one bedroom, 2 bedrooms, or mansion. What you've built and what you're building on is not ordinary. See, that's the part as well. People forget that in order to build you have to build on something. That sleeping on your friend's couch, moving back in with your parents, staying in a one bedroom. That's the build on part right there, that's what you're building on. I had no room. I lived out of my car for about a year; I wouldn't dare move my clothes anywhere. Just a straight nomad, wherever I stayed, I would go outside, get my one outfit out of the car, shower, and go. I had people who opened their doors up to me, but it wasn't meant for me to build on that, because I refused everyone who did. It was meant for me to build on living out of my car, and right now I'm writing this book from a one bedroom, still building. I remember when I was going through that living out of my car stage, I had a friend invite me to his big weekend birthday bash in Houston. I mean, people was flying in from everywhere Georgia, New Jersey, New York, California, some I knew, some I didn't we was like fifty deep, if not more. Anyway, I pulled up to the penthouse, and my people were outside to greet me. I saw my bro's face; he didn't say anything at the time, but I knew what he was thinking. He waited until we got alone and pulled me to the side like "Yo bro what's going on, that hurt my heart seeing all your clothes and belongings in the car like that". I understood where he was coming from, but he didn't know that's what I was building on. I had a friend who let me stay with him for 2 months until my apartment was ready, he told me numerous times "Man bring your clothes in the house Man", but he didn't know that's what I was building on. So being in this one bedroom, becoming a grandfather, I'm here to tell you what I built thus far isn't ordinary, what I built on isn't ordinary, and what I'm still building is not going to be ordinary. You'll hear a lot more about how I ended up living out of my car and more at a later date. You need to know what you've built, what you're building on, and what you're still building isn't going to be ordinary. Also, always remember what ordinary means, ordinary means normal, standard, common, not unusual. Now you tell me if what you have built is ordinary...

Reader's Thoughts

It's not about If

You're Gonna Win

It's About The

Way

You're Gonna Win

I'm going to start this off like this, we were born to win, point, blank, period. If you don't believe you were born to win, you need to rethink some things, because you were. It's not always going to look like the win, because wins go like this. First, the win is in transit, which means it's on the way, then the win goes into progress, which means its developing, and then the win goes to complete mode, which means the win is all yours. I remember a rapper saying it's levels to this, and he was right, because it really is levels to this. That's why I said it's not about if you're going to win, it's about how you're going to win, because it's all a process, and the process is the way you're going to win. Back in 1997 and don't calculate my years people, but back in "97" I was on a first-time football championship team for my high school, no other team had ever won a championship for our school, in order to get there, we had to know it wasn't about if we were going to win, it was about the way we were going to win. Down 28 to 6 at half time, we came out in the second half of the game and dominated. My best brother, yes once again the one who was held at gun point with me, put the team on his back. My bro had 25 carries for 272 yards and 3 touchdowns, leading us to a 34-31 victory. We only allowed 3 points in that 2nd half. I'm simply saying you don't ever know how you're going to win, even when it's looking like a loss, believe me it's not. I'm not saying we don't take losses, because we all have. My thing is I don't care if it looks like a loss, keep going for the win.

Sometimes You Have
To Add To Your Value
By Subtracting

When reading this, it seems simple, but it's hard to subtract things you don't want to subtract. Sometimes we don't even care about our values because we love what we don't want to let go of so much. I'll be the first to tell you, it took me forever to subtract some things, to be honest I'm still subtracting. You know one of the things I knew is that I had to subtract the most meaningless conversations on the phone with people. Some of those conversations would go on for two or three hours, I had to wake up and tell myself, "Come on man do you know how much you could have gotten accomplished in those hours". You know what my motto is to this as long as I don't subtract my love for the Great I AM, my health, my faith, my honesty, my loyalty, my beautiful thoughts, my kind ways, my useful words, my energetic spirit, my optimism, my love for others, my uplift, my ability to do what I can, my willingness to share and help, my compassion, my consideration, my perseverance, my understanding, my fairness, my accountability, my go get it mentality, my willingness to learn and teach then my value is still intact and looking to be increased. That list could of went on forever, but I'd thought I would stop there. We all know sometimes you have to subtract people, tv, social media, conversations, availability, meaningless relationships, bad thoughts, false beliefs, pessimism, lack of faith, laziness, lack of drive, bad habits. This list can go on forever, too, because there are many things that you must subtract in order to add to your value. I'm excited to read and hear about some of the things you feel should be subtracted to add to one's value.

May The Worse
Days Of Your Future
Still Be Better Than
The Best Days Of
Your Past

You got to think this, you got to know this, you got to fight for this, you got to own this. I'm pretty sure all of us have been sick and tired of bad days, we've all had our fair share, although there's no such thing as bad days as long as you're breathing, well that's what they say. I'm here to tell you emotions run deep, and that's what bad days revolve around, emotions. You have to remember, you have the steering wheel when it comes to your emotions; any negative emotion that tries to sneak up on you, steer it away. I studied this, I researched this, and it wasn't just about this saying; I researched ways to acquire this and make it count in your life, and it all came back to emotions. You know what else it led me to, it led me to people that were homeless, people that were poor, people that didn't have much and then became a success. Why it led me to this is because those people tend to remember the best days of their past more often than people that didn't have a huge struggle, those that were profoundly blessed in their past tend to have had so many best days that it can be overwhelming to remember them all verses those that had more struggles, those people tend to remember all their best days more vividly, hopefully you comprehend what I'm saying. No matter how your past was and how it is for you now, I just want you to know from me to you, may the worst days of your future still be better than the best days of your past. This simply means you have some beautiful days ahead of you, enjoy them with nothing but beautiful emotions.

Your Job Isn't Your
Purpose It's Your Financial
Drive To Your Purpose

This isn't for everybody, because some people's jobs are their purpose. I completely understand that, and I also understand that there are people out there who just don't want to use their job for a financial drive to their purpose; they just want to work a 9 to 5 and be done with it, I completely understand that too. Yet though this is for a lot of us, including me. We all have a purpose, and it's not always revealed in the first 20, 30, 40 years of your expiring experience (life), but it's there, and when it is revealed, I encourage you so much to use that 9 to 5 as your own personal financial driver. This means save as much as you can to acquire that purpose, spend as little as you can to acquire that purpose, go to work, and just go home to acquire that purpose, less hanging out to acquire that purpose. When I say some people's jobs are their purpose, I'm not necessarily talking about Heart surgeons, doctors, nurses, or anyone in the medical field, for that matter, I'm not necessarily talking about preachers, teachers, athletes, etc. The reason I'm not necessarily talking about them is that I can guarantee you some of them had to use a 9 to 5 for a financial drive to their purpose, which is teaching, preaching, healing, entertaining, etc. I'm sure a lot of them had to work to pay for their education, had to work and save to get their own church or had to work to pay the church bills that they own, that's some examples of a financial drive to your purpose. Some one that I tend to study, not listen to, study. It's the difference between listening to and studying that means the world. Listening to is listening, studying is learning, remember that. He goes by the name of Keion Henderson, some of you may not know him, some of you might, some of you may not like him, some of you may. Some may know him as Shaq's ex-wife husband, and if you know him as that I'm going to tell you one thing, Shaunie scored enough for me to know her as Shaunie Henderson, that's it that's all(not sure what they are now today). Anyway, I'll always remember a story he told. Being Senior Pastor, he had his own church in Fort Wayne, Indiana, started it actually. He called his mother and told her that the Great I Am ordered his steps to move to Houston, Tx; in which, he did what he was told to do and went to be an assistant to another Senior Pastor. He got to Houston and didn't have anywhere to stay. He stated that the pastor of the church he was going to be an assistant at found him an apartment and paid for it until he got on his feet. This the part right here, he went on to say that he found a job making $52,000 a year, then got another after that one making $104,000 a year. When he started the job making $104,000 a year, he still lived like he was making $52,000 a year. He didn't up his lifestyle because his income went up, he stashed the other $52,000, and when he went to close on the new church for the people, he was $60,000 short, well we all know where that came from that $52,000 that he had been stashing using his 9 to 5.

This is the perfect example that your job isn't your purpose; it's your financial drive to your purpose. Right now, today Keion Henderson is Senior Pastor of the Light House Church in Houston, Texas. I definitely Recommend you check him out, of course he's not perfect, but he's a real one. That story alone should tell you that. I hope this encourages someone that is just working a 9 to 5 just to work, to work that 9 to 5 all the way to their purpose and ride out in cruise control on Purpose Highway!!!

I don't judge people, I don't look down on people, that's just me, and I'm not trying to make myself look good in this book, it just is what it is, and that's what it is. I'm not telling you what to do, I'm just encouraging you that if you don't want to work your 9 to 5 for 40 or 50 years, use it for a financial drive to do what it is you love that will benefit you and the ones you love.

You Can't Be

A

Random You

I have to be honest, when I wrote this down, it had my mind going in circles. I couldn't figure out what my thoughts were telling me, and then it came to me. Everyone reading this book, I'm sure, has had encounters with random people, what's so crazy is that I also figured we even have encounters with a random us, which is a random you. This rambled through my mind so much that I had to send out a meaning behind it when I sent it out on November 28th, 2023, and that's the only time I have ever done that. That meaning went like this, you know, when people say "oh I just asked some random people," you can't ask a random you, you have to ask you what am I doing right, what am I doing wrong? That's all I could come up with at the time. I now know when you answer those two questions and follow through with your answers, that's how you get back to the pure you, but the more and more I thought about it all types of thoughts began to form, and one of them contradicts this saying. I began to think you can be a random you. The reason I say this is because we were all born so pure, so clean. When we were first born, we didn't know the ways of the world. As time went on, we began to pick up so many characteristics of our environments, so many habits that surrounded us, we all just became unclean and random people to our own selves. I don't care who you are; you picked up something that is of this world and not of the Great I Am along the way. That's why I tend to say you can be a random you, but it's not good, so you shouldn't be a random you, and you can't be a random you, because you can't afford to be a random you. Being a random you can cost you your life. Not knowing who you really are is dangerous. Whatever you do, if you're in a stage of your life where you know you're a random you right now, I recommend you fight hard to get back to the pure you. You didn't do drugs when you were born you were pure, you didn't drink alcohol when you were born you were pure, you didn't watch porn when you were born you were pure, you didn't steal when you were born you were pure, you didn't lie when you were born you were pure, you didn't use profanity when you were born you were pure, you didn't commit adultery when you were born you were pure, this list can go on showing us how pure we were when we were born. So, what we all need to understand is that we can't be a random you, because it won't get us to where we are going. We must give it all we have to get back to our pure selves and explain to others that it's not safe being a random you. I'll sum this up by saying you can be a random you, but you shouldn't be a random you unless you're being a positive force random you that no one is used to, now that's the perfect way to go if you're going to be a random you.

You Never Know
Who's With You
Until They Have
The Option Not
To Be

It's beautiful to have a team, it's beautiful to have people on your side, it's beautiful to have family. All those things give you a sense of support, but it sure is tough when family members, a teammate, or someone by your side decides they don't want to be a part of you anymore. That's where this comes in at, "You never know who's with you until they have the option not to be". The key word is option, because when one is faced with an option, that simply means they must make a decision, and you're not always the choice. Confusion comes when options arise; remember that. Not only does confusion come to the person faced with the choice, but it also comes to you as well, because it leaves you asking the question why? I say this with confidence, don't ask yourself why. When someone makes a decision and you're not a part of that decision, you have to simply tell yourself they're not with me, and you also have to remind yourself that you did something good previously that made that person want to be with you. Look at your goodness, because I'm sure 9 times out of 10, you probably did something they didn't like or have a habit that they're tired of, whatever it was that made them not choose you, you don't worry about that, keep looking at your goodness regardless of anything. I remember a friend of mine's father passed away. Before he passed away, I used to hear so many people talk down on this man and turn their back on him. They weren't choosing him at all. I had the honor of speaking at his funeral. Guess what, I seen all those people I heard talking down on him and about him at his funeral. For some reason, that did something to me, I don't even know how to explain it. When I took the stage, I told them, this man was good to everyone in here at some point in his life, or you all would of not ever allowed him in your life. I went on to say, won't you all think about all the good things he did for you, won't you think about the times he did something to make you love him, because everyone in here loved him at some point in your life. People tend to forget about the goodness of people; that's why it's important to remind yourself of the goodness in you, because people catch amnesia quickly. Me personally, I cannot and will not hold hatred in my heart for anyone, no matter what they did to me. I just have that type of loyalty in me. That's one thing nobody can say is that I turned my back on them. Every time I've been faced with the dilemma you never know who's with you until they have the option not to be I've always stuck it out with my people, because my people are never an option, and you're not either.

Sometimes Rejection

Is Protection

I was done writing for tonight, just left this title on the page for tomorrow, no stories y'all. Just sat down to watch some basketball, make a couple phone calls, and relax, just me and my niece GIA, who's 2 years old (the most beautiful dog ever). All of a sudden, this video entered my presence. It was a video of a friend of mine, I went to high school with and grew up with in the hood. Straight up, I saw my boy scrapping and struggling when we were younger, as we all were, but everybody struggles not the same. He wasn't a part of my main brothers, but we were always alright. It was cool to me to see him give himself to the Mystery, to the Great I Am. I see the word minister in front of his name now. I love that. I use to see people, you know people who thought they were to cool, or people who might just have you around for a certain reason, have him around and reject him; never the less, people will probably say well Anton you were a part of both of those types of crowds, which I probably was and that's probably why I noticed it, but I didn't ever rock like that and neither did my brothers, and when I say rock like that, that means we didn't do that. It dawned on me, though, that it was beautiful that they were rejecting him, because where we grew up, it's so easy to get sucked in; it's best you be rejected by certain crowds that you think may be the in crowd. I truly believe that if he were accepted by those crowds, he probably wouldn't be as close to the Great I Am as he is, because it's facts a lot of us who were rolling in those crowds are not. The video that was playing it just showed pictures of him with a song playing in the background; it was cool. The song and what I remember of him matched up perfectly. The song isn't a new song, but go check it out, it's titled "I'm still standing by Evelyn Foxx. What we all need to understand is that rejection is a covering. Most people don't like to be rejected, because it's an uncomfortable feeling, until you realize you're being protected. I've seen so many of my friends be rejected, it's ridiculous. I'll speak about my rejections another time, and yeah, they were ridiculous just like there's. I'm just thankful that none of us ever felt like it was the Great I am that was rejecting us, when you grow up without the belief that can sometimes seep into people's minds. Just because you may not have what others have or be accepted like others are accepted doesn't mean you're being rejected by the Mystery; it simply means you're being prepped. I'm a firm believer in preparation. Always remember, not only is rejection sometimes protection, but rejection is also redirection.

Be Faithful

To

Your Focus

I guess a lot of people would say this is easier said than done. Well, I would say when you're tapped in, you're tapped in. We all know it's not easy to tap in; it takes a different type of drive, a different type of energy, which we all possess. It's not more so about your focus than it is your faithfulness. This is what we all must understand being faithful to the focus is what enhances the focus. The focus can be there, but if the faithfulness isn't, which simply means the consistency and commitment to the focus, then the focus is diluted, tampered with, and not pure. There are so many things on this earth that require 100% focus if you want to attain what it is your focus is on. When my children are speaking to me, I give them my 100% focus; I don't care what's going on around me, I'm not giving them a diluted focus. This is the mindset necessary to be faithful to your focus. You know one thing I've noticed is that when my friends went to prison, they all came out of prison with something they've accomplished. I have a friend that is a certified electrician out of prison, I have a brother and cousin that acquired their GED out of prison, I have a friend that's a certified welder out of prison, and I have a friend who read himself right into his own business out of prison. I say all of that to say this, they were faithful to their focus. I don't know what the outcomes would have been if they were free, but I do know that being away from the outside world definitely helped them be more faithful to their focus and accomplish the goals that they set out for themselves. Find what it is that you want to focus on and be faithful to it. I can guarantee you, you will love the outcome.

Love Being

Underestimated

I love this because I went through this as a little boy, I mean, probably not even 5 years old yet, and it never left me. I didn't ever forget. Just know everything that I write in this book is true and 100% facts. Now, at the time, I didn't know what underestimating was, but I did know how to comprehend when someone didn't think I was worthy or capable of doing something. I have an uncle (through marriage, my aunt's husband), and I say have, because he's still alive today. I don't know what it was, but he took it upon himself to call me retard every time he called me, every time he spoke to me or about me, every time he saw me; that was my name from him to me. No one else ever called me that, and I never understood why no one would ever stop him or say something to him about calling me that, and this man was legit serious in thinking I was a retard; nevertheless, the way I feel, no one on this earth is a retard. So, I knew at a young age how he felt about me and how he characterized me. I took that like a champ, didn't ever allow it to mess with my self-esteem or confidence, carried on with life like the G that I am, real soldier, built way stronger than ford tough. It was nothing that man or no man, for that matter, could do to destroy me. As I got older and learned what people definition of a retard was, that gave me even more drive not to prove anything to him, but to prove to me what I'm capable of. The Great I Am is so funny, it's out of control, the mystery always seems to tickle me with its humor, and I just pay attention and laugh; it talks right in front of our faces every day. So, this is how this joke went. I'm not saying my uncle was or is my enemy, but anybody who calls you retard and means it, they might be. In that great book (The Basic Instructions Before Leaving Earth-B.I.B.L.E), it states that he will prepare a table before me in the presence of my enemies. It was a joyful feeling when my uncle had to watch me graduate from college on the Dean's list with my Bachelor of Science in Business Administration and my minor in accounting. I would really like to know what was going through his mind when he heard my name called and watched me walk across that stage to receive my degree, seriously I would really love to know that. I have not ever brought this up, because I didn't ever feel the need to, but I can honestly say that it helped me to love being underestimated. So, the next time you know that you're being underestimated, be faithful to your focus and go get yours.

Allow Me To

Be A Liability Until

I Can Become An

Asset

I had a few people who didn't like this when I sent it out, actually, this was probably the only one that got some dislikes, to be honest. That didn't matter to me, though, because I understood who wants to be a liability. Me personally I'm humble enough that if I had to be a liability and I have been one before, I'm willing until the time presents itself to move to the next level. The reason a lot of people don't like this is that it means that someone else is liable for you, and that can be embarrassing, especially for adults. I'll tell you one thing, that person or persons who allows you to be a liability until you become an asset, please love on them and give them the highest respect possible, because that's not an easy thing to do. See, when you're considered a liability, people tend to look at you as useless; they look at you as if you're at a disadvantage to whatever it is they may have going on, versus when you're an asset people look at you as useful and valuable. As I stated earlier in this book, I'm a fan and supporter of Keion Henderson's hard work. I actually learned this from him, and I thought it was so humble with humility. I found myself in this place so many times in the past that I could 100% relate to what he was saying from my understanding T.D. Jakes was one of Keion's mentors. So, before he became famous himself, he didn't have much to give, so this was a key question that he asked pastor Jakes "Would he allow him to be a liability until he can become an asset?" It was just so amazing to me to hear a man put himself at such a standard. I told myself I will not ever be afraid to ask someone this question if need be. It's ok to be a liability sometimes, we don't always have it the way we would like it and it's understandable to people who know what it's like to be in a certain situation. You know the first assistant job that Keion got the pastor that took him in allowed him to be a liability until he became an asset. Now some years later those people that did him those favors can definitely say it was all worth it, because he's now one of the biggest assets to come out of the spiritual field. If you're ever in a position where you have to be a liability, be humble enough to be one and strong enough to fight your way to being an asset.

Be Specific With
The Seed That You're
Going To Sew

I understand that a lot of people don't know much about seed sewing. I was definitely one of those people, and it's true to say that the first seed I ever sewed, I didn't even know I was sewing it, let alone being specific about it. I want to tell you all that seed sewing really works. When I finally educated myself on it, I began to be specific, and the specifications began to show themselves. Was I in disbelief? No, was I amazed? Yes. I was amazed just to know that we have this gift, and this power, it's just amazing. I told you all about the seed I sewed from jail. I wasn't specific about that, but that seed I sewed to land a job, the mystery made sure to reveal to me to be specific. That's when I learned to be specific about the seeds that I sowed. Ever since that revelation occurred, I have always encouraged people to be specific, and I've had plenty of people come to me and say, "YO Bro that worked." All I could look and say is you know who to thank, and it's not me. So please to you all, if you're a believer and even if you're not a believer, teach your children early about sowing seeds so they can see on their own the goodness of the power and the gift they are blessed with.

Strength Is
Coming Where You
Need It

It's important that we always know this. To all the adults reading this book, please explain to the younger ones that strength always comes on time. Also, let them know that there is not a time in your life that you've dealt with a weakness, and it wasn't filled with strength. I will tell all of us like I told myself when I told myself this, we can't know strength without weakness, and we can't know weakness without strength, that's just a known fact. Does it sound cliché? Sure, it does, but I can guarantee you that it's 100 percent true. Perfect example, I have a sister who has nine children and two grandchildren. My sister had gotten into some trouble and had to go away for a good while. I watched my nieces and nephews cry and show a weakness that there was nothing I could do about. I knew deep down inside that that weakness would be filled with strength one day, but they didn't know that. I have a video of my nieces and nephews being surprised by their mother coming home after a whole year. Boy, if they didn't learn about a weakness getting filled with strength. I can assure you that the video will bring tears to your eyes. I took it upon myself to teach them right then and there about weakness getting filled with strength, and I can tell they understood what I was talking about, because I used a life experience that they faced to teach them. If we don't do anything, let's always teach strength, it's important.

Reader's Thoughts

Play Your Part

Because

Every Part Is

Significant

First off, let's make sure we understand the word significant, that is a very powerful word. Significant is to have importance, significant is to have a special meaning, a meaning that lets you know you are larger than life in many ways. It means you are great; you are worthy of attention. I'm just going to say important, important, important, your part is. It's always important to know your part; that's what makes you and the part you play significant, knowing your part. One of my brothers committed a murder and had to go away to prison for 10 years; it took a toll on all of us, especially his son. I knew right away what my part was as soon as my brother was sentenced. I knew my part was significant, so I took it very seriously. I took on the part of making sure my nephew/God son, who was only about 3 or 4 years old at the time, was going to graduate high school and that he was going to be alright no matter what. I made sure I got him every summer, and as much as I could for that matter. I made sure I made all his important school events that I could, although I lived in another state, I walked with him on his senior day. I just made sure I did all the things to let him know he had support and a man in his life who cared for him.

I didn't go overboard and try to be his father, because I knew that was impossible, so I made sure I played my part to the best of my ability and let everyone else play their part. My nephew still faced some battles, but I can honestly say the part I was created to play got him through high school and allowed him to walk into manhood as his own man. Please always remember that your role is always important, no matter what that role is; know it's significant.

Don't Allow The
Broken Parts Of You To
Speak To The Parts That's
Still Together

I hope this doesn't go over your head. I hope everyone fully comprehends this. Of course, I feel like everything in this book is important when it comes to being on this earth and creating happiness that even knows how to fight sadness and brokenness. We all know that we're not always 100% happy, we're not always 100% together, and that's totally fine. What's not totally fine is when you let those weak areas begin to talk to the strong areas, and you know your strong areas. Here's a metaphor I was a lousy English student, just couldn't get it together, but I will not ever allow my lousiness in English to affect my strength in Math, if that makes sense to you. I would not ever say I'm no good in English, so there's no way I will ever be good in math. To make even more sense of it, look at me now up here writing a book. That lets you know that I didn't allow my brokenness to speak to my strengths, nor did I allow my brokenness to stay broken either.So why are you not allowing the broken parts to speak to the parts that are still together? Make sure you put the broken parts together. Writing this book showed me that I put my broken parts together. Apply this to your life. I know sometimes we're broken in the financial area, but strong in love. It was one year I had no form of income and no money to my name; I allowed that to talk to my love, the area in which I knew I was strong in. This is how I know I allowed it to talk to my love; this is the only time in my life that I wanted to take my own life, because I couldn't provide for my children. I am so thankful I made it through that phase, because I was allowing my broken parts to speak to the parts that were still together. Fight for your togetherness and create that happiness that

Your Gift Speaks

For a lot of us, our gifts are speaking, and we don't even know it. I can honestly say I feel as if I'm guilty of this. I have heard numerous people speak on a gift they say I possess, and it's always the same gift, but different people saying it. I have been in Texas and been told about this gift I have, I have been in New York and have been told about this gift I have, I have been in North and South Carolina and have been told about this gift I have, I have been in Arkansas and have been told about this gift I have and as I stated it's always from different people. So, you can't tell me your gift doesn't speak. Just take the time to listen, and I guarantee you, you will hear it, and once you hear it, put your gift to work and make it louder.

Welcome To Uplift

Part Two

If you haven't read part one, I would highly recommend it, just so you can get a better overview of how 'Welcome to Uplift' came all about. I would like to thank everyone who supported part one, and I want to thank everyone right now who is supporting part two. I'm a firm believer in teaching children while they're young about whatever it is that life throws our way. We don't have to wait until they're 13 years old to begin to be authentic with them about the ins and outs of what goes on in everyday life. It may be too late, and they may have already created their own perception of life, so please know these books are kid friendly and please share with the youth. It's what they need; they need to know they can make it through difficult situations with strength, happiness, optimism, perseverance, and the confidence that everything is going to work itself out. I will continue to always write welcome to uplift, even if it's just my daughter, son, and grandson reading it, it will always be here for my family, and I pray you all trust my words to always be there for your families. Welcome To Uplift!!!!

Some Beautiful

Sudden 'Lys Are On The

Way

Most of the time, when we hear the word suddenly, we think of something that just happened immediately without warning, and most of the time, it deals with something negative. Well, when this came to me, I immediately started thinking about all the beautiful things that's on the way that I don't know about, and how it's going to happen so suddenly, believe me when I tell you, you have some beautiful sudden 'Lys on the way. My little brother right now is in prison serving 11 years for attempted murder; regardless of what he did, he has some beautiful sudden 'Lys on the way. You just imagine how those women and men in prison feel when that release day comes, and they're just sitting there waiting for their name to be called, they don't know what time it's going to be, but they know it's on schedule to be called, and then suddenly their name is called. It must be one of the best feelings ever to know you're being set free and given a chance to accept some more beautiful sudden 'Lys. So just always keep in mind you have some beautiful sudden 'Lys on the way, even when it looks as if it's not.

YOUR HUG MIGHT

BE THE FIRST

HUG THEY RECEIVED

ALL WEEK. YOUR HIGHFIVE

MIGHT BE THE FIRST HIGHFIVE

THEY RECEIVED ALL WEEK.

YOUR TOUCH HAS POWER